(UN)BELONGING

By the same author

Preparations for Depature (2017)
Cult (2016)
Distance (2014)
Suburban Exile (2011)
Symptoms of Homesickness (2010)

(UN)BELONGING

NATHANAEL O'REILLY

RECENT
WORK
PRESS

(Un)belonging
Recent Work Press
Canberra, Australia

Copyright © Nathanael O'Reilly, 2020

ISBN: 9780648685333 (paperback)

 A catalogue record for this book is available from the National Library of Australia

All rights reserved. This book is copyright. Except for private study, research, criticism or reviews as permitted under the Copyright Act, no part of this book may be reproduced, stored in a retrieval system, or transmitted in any form by any means without prior written permission. Enquiries should be addressed to the publisher.

Cover image: 'Great Smokey Mountains, Gatlinburg, USA' by Ashwin Patel on Unsplash
Cover design: Recent Work Press
Set by Recent Work Press

recentworkpress.com

MD

For Tricia & Celeste

Contents

Your Gaze	3
Exploring the Neighborhood After Ten Days Confined at Home Due to Surgery	5
O My America!	6
Surgery Waiting Room	7
Well Tempered	9
The Boy from Hope	12
The Confessions of Donald J. Trump	13
Answers	16
Études	17
Grand Canal Drowning	19
Parklife	20
Icelandic Evening	21
Nativity	22
Rain Delay	23
Americans	24
Maître D'	25
Serenade	26
In the Backstreet	27
Tattooed	28
Cave and Cohen	29
Autumn Spring	30
Hiraeth	32
(Un)belonging	33
Booranga Sonnets	35
Kengal	49
School Days	50
Too Young	52
Saronic	53
Return Flight	57
Ash Wednesday	59
Blackout	60

Mort	61
Pond Frog	62
Alt-facts Bio	63
Escape Sonnet	64
Refuge	65
Nonchalance	66
Decay	67
Pecos	68
Ice Cream Social	69
Swinging	70
The Third of July	71
Back Verandah Dinner	72
As He Lies Dying	73
Beach Ballet	75

... You are neither here nor there,
A hurry through which known and strange things pass ...

> Seamus Heaney
> (from 'Postscript')

I had my existence. I was there.
Me in place and the place in me.

> Seamus Heaney
> (from 'A Herbal')

Your Gaze

Yesterday I found a photograph
taken in nineteen eighty-eight

on the oval after school. You wore
a green tartan skirt, a white blouse,

black stockings, a bottle-green blazer
and black Clarks school shoes.

Your gaze ignores the camera,
focuses on the plains north

of school where we roamed
on winter afternoons until twilight,

watched rabbits bound towards
their burrows and kangaroos

descend upon the creek to drink,
the plains where sheep grazed

upon lush grass while we lay
together in a hollow sheltered

from the westerly, your auburn
hair curtaining our faces, apricot

scent of shampoo in my nostrils,
your tongue in my mouth, hands

inside my woollen jumper,
the plains erased from the map

in ninety-nine when bulldozers
scraped the landscape, destroyed

all vegetation and the new suburb
was erected: cul-de-sacs, boulevards,

courts, crescents, quarter-acre blocks,
brick-veneer houses, Colorbond fences,

concrete footpaths and backyard pools.
In the photograph, your gaze writes

an invisible history only we can read.

Exploring the Neighborhood After Ten Days Confined at Home Due to Surgery

Three flags fly above the Baptist church
ready for July Fourth. The sign proclaims
THIS SUNDAY: PATRIOTIC SERMON.

A new girl named Tatiana rings up
my six-pack of IPA and salt and vinegar
chips at Brookshire's supermarket.

My favourite neighbor has swapped
his Land Rover for a Suburban,
losing his hint of European cool.

Three more houses are for sale
or lease and Matt across the street
has just mown and edged his lawn.

The woman with pink personalized
license plates proclaiming OIL WFE
is moving out, leaving trash behind.

The baseball fields, basketball
courts and playground are deserted,
kids trapped indoors by heat.

Old Ray on Olympic watches the street
on a white plastic chair in his open garage,
Katie panting faithfully by his side.

Empty recycling bins lie helpless
on their sides waiting for fathers
to come home and carry them inside.

O My America!

An overweight, bearded middle-aged
black man wearing a baseball cap,
t-shirt and cargo shorts spreads
his stocky legs wide, leans forward
over the trunk of his Ford Focus sedan
parked in the driveway of his suburban
middle-class four-bedroom brick home,
hands behind his head, fingers locked,
as an overweight, bearded middle-aged
white cop wearing a handgun and Taser
moves his open hands over the suspect's
body, maintains a spoken commentary:
license my roving hands and let them go
before, behind, between, above, below.
O my America, my newfoundland!

Surgery Waiting Room

HGTV plays on the wall-mounted
flatscreen in the dermatologist's
waiting room. Elderly patients

bicker with spouses over petty issues,
watch videos on their phones of grandkids
with the volume maxed out, oblivious

to the preferences of others. Patients
sport bandages advertising sites
of excisions from ears, cheeks, foreheads and scalps.

Unsteady hands and weak eyes puzzle over
the newfangled coffee machine until the youngest
patient (only forty-three!) steps in, takes orders,

makes coffee for his elders. The television
sells materialistic fantasies of aesthetic glories,
enviable residences at reasonable prices,

bargains under list price with minimal renovations
required. *Just five hundred grand move-in ready!*
The botoxed, bleached-toothed, spray-tanned

hosts gesticulate and gush over glistening kitchens
and bathrooms: *We will make this your dream home!*
Tremulous elderly patients watch, listen, nod

assent, declare *AIN'T THAT PRETTY, HONEY?!*
The nurse returns, adopts a sympathetic expression,
sighs ... *Well Sir, it looks like we're going to have*

to go back and take off another layer. The patient's
wife interjects - *I guess it's a good thing you mowed
the lawn and fed the cat. You'd better go and pee -*

7

while couples on HGTV attempt to assemble
a crib in preparation for their firstborn. An old
man shakes his head, mutters *Well, that was a stupid ad*

to his wife snoring in the recliner beside him.
On the other side of the wall the surgeon's scalpel
slices skin, excavates through layers, eliminates

cancerous cells, cuts down towards healthy tissue.
An accompanying spouse shakes her head
theatrically, sighs like a deflating balloon -

It takes longer to get sewn up than it does to get cut!

Well Tempered

Co-written with Lachlan Brown

Prelude: Instructions for Travel

When facing
a veritable quandary
insert hormone pellets

Gather the mob
at the bicycle
assembly point

Wish for a book at Powell's
locate fancy beasts, a mosquito
cry *hallelujah!* then blackout

Imagine noir script starring
woman in red trench coat
coming in out of the rain

Take a pre-dawn taxi
to Central. Catch a country
train to Wagga Wagga

Shuffle to the buffet
car like Cliff Young.
Another poet always ahead

Play pool & the pokies
& belt out AC/DC karaoke
at the St. Mary's leagues club

Search Sorbonne bookstores
for an English translation
of *Les Fleurs du Mal*

Slip feet into shoes
like a character
in Murray Bail's *Homesickness*

Check bags from DFW to PDX
return seats to upright positions
wash hands before everything

Eat pub grub with JJ. Bring
BC coffee. Share the means
of production with AA

Fugue: Second Western

the symmetry of action/inaction means that
a Portland Prius and a Fort Worth pickup
will cancel each other out, but you keep going

west young man, keep tightening the buckle
on your Bible belt 'cause that thing's gotta hold
against the breaking drought against the clean

air corridors that threaten to rupture and pour
across this continent. I can't believe that yours
is the only house in the neighbourhood without

a gun. Here, I've added one to your basket
you can bumper sticker this moment later
after you ride the bull/drink the whiskey/

sing a national anthem (choose one). Even
with drilled oil you can't always get where
you want. In this town there are bus timetables

with holes so large that Lear jets are flying
through them. Lear Jets! *Ave, Rex Caeli*

And thank you sponsors for making every-
thing possible and also for the freedom
to choose unique flavours. Such as the Iraq.
Such as the Corona in best position i.e. inverted

and pouring itself into a margarita like a
clepsydrian apocalypse. You are personally
welcome, sir, but leave your constitutionally

monarchic ideas back in your own country.
And don't come crying to me if some
liberal NPR-loving shyster tells you off when

your kids are noisy in a public place. Consider
this your first warning. There are people with
weird beliefs. There are decrees which we all

obey. There is a Segway like Apollo's chariot
sliding across a white square, reminding you
to wear pants as the fountain shoots skywards.

The Boy from Hope

Between Texarkana and Arkadelphia
Clinton's childhood home stands in Hope—
unoccupied, boarded-up and run-down,
with an overgrown backyard
and views of a railway line,
a busy four-lane highway
and a rustic convenience store.
Still, one could imagine little Bill
tottering about on the front porch
taking the first steps towards
a remarkable career, watched casually
by his grandparents and widowed mother,
none of whom could possibly have imagined
what kind of man he would become—
brilliant, feared, admired, hated and flawed,
shades of Hamlet and Macbeth.

A visitor's center now occupies
the house next door to Bill's,
containing photographs and texts,
plus the obligatory gift shop beside
the exit. After checking out pictures
of Bill as a child in Hope and Hot Springs
and a bearded, long-haired young man
at Georgetown, Oxford and Yale, I pass
on the souvenirs and cross the highway
to buy a cigar and a fifth of whiskey.

The Confessions of Donald J. Trump

Well, the leaks are real.
I mean, the leaks are real.
The leaks are absolutely real.

The news is fake because
so much of the news is fake.
I was coming into office.

I want to find a friendly reporter.
Are you a friendly reporter?
Now, that's what I call a nice question.

We had a very, very big margin.
By the way, it would be great
if we could get along with Russia.

I'm not ranting and raving.
I'm just telling you.
You know, you're dishonest people.

But, but I'm not ranting and raving.
I love this. I'm having a good time
doing it. I don't mind bad stories.

Look, I want to see an honest press.
Yes, oh, this is going to be
a bad question, but that's OK.

It would be the electric chair.
OK? He should be put in the electric …
You would even call for the institution of the death penalty.

I see tone. You know the word tone.
The tone is such hatred.
And it's all about unification.

And he has had a tremendous career.
And he will be I think a fantastic addition.
Some people are so surprised

that we're having strong borders.
I'm not going to tell you anything
about what I'm going to do.

I'm not going to talk about military stuff.
I don't have to tell you
what I'm going to do in North Korea.

Nuclear holocaust
would be like no other
and I'll get killed ...

I don't have to tell you.
Your ratings aren't as good
as some of the other people that are waiting.

To be honest, I inherited a mess,
a mess, at home and abroad, a mess.
The stock market has hit record numbers.

Tremendous disservice.
The level of dishonesty is out of control.
We're going to take care of it all.

Hillary Clinton did a reset,
remember with the stupid plastic button
that made us all look like a bunch of jerks?

And the wall is going to be a great wall
and it's going to be a wall negotiated by me.
Every country takes advantage of us almost.

I guess it was the biggest
electoral college win since Ronald Reagan.
This administration is running like a fine-tuned machine,
despite the fact that I can't get my cabinet approved.
President Putin called me up very nicely
to congratulate me on the win of the election.

I have nothing to do with Russia.
I told you, I have no deals there,
I have no anything.

Answers

A lone slightly-crushed blue M&M
rests on the classroom's grey carpet
between rows of wooden chairs.

A student writes with her right hand
while inserting two fingers of her left
into her mouth, withdrawing pink gum.

Cheeks rest on fists. Fingertips scratch
stubble, tuck hair behind ears. Muscles
suck mucus back into nostrils.

Knees bounce as hands move blue
pens left to right across lined paper.
Eyes glance at the clock. Students cough

into collars and elbows, adjust ponytails,
reverse black baseball caps, rotate wrists,
crack knuckles, search for answers

in the green magnolia boughs outside
the window, on the cream ceiling tiles,
amongst leaves of grass on manicured lawns.

Études

I
Pre-dawn embraces
impress like détente.

II
Raspberry tea steeps,
sacrificing heat.

III
I read *High Windows*
on the train to Hull,
contemplate fuck-ups.

IV
A bikini-clad woman
rinses in the open shower
beside the hotel pool
watching males gaze.

V
The woman at the café
in the Slovakian railway
station doesn't understand
bread, brot, pane or *pain*—
I depart hungry.

VI
Warning signs on the train
are posted in five languages—
not one my native tongue.

VII
I stand in the bar carriage,
legs wide like a sailor in rough
seas, riding every curve's
sway, saving precious liquid.

VIII
Icicles melt from rose bushes,
drip upon dead black leaves.

IX
The front desk worker
and a sweaty member
sing along to Men
at Work's Down Under
in a Texas YMCA.

X
Feijoa halves mixed with sugar
tumble in boiling water.

Grand Canal Drowning

My great-great-grandfather drowned
in the Grand Canal on his way home
from the pub. Great-uncle Sean told
the story, laughing at the absurdity
of a six-three man drowning in a canal
only five-ten deep. Stumbling across
dark fields towards his sleeping family,
the Guinness he'd put away combined
with the cloudy night didn't give him
a chance. He plunged face-first
into the water, swallowed a dirty pint
in surprise, never found his feet.

One hundred and twenty years
later, I set out to hike the Grand
Canal from Dublin to the Shannon.
On the third day, Ireland's hottest
on record, I stood stranded
on the wrong side of the water,
blocked by blackthorn thickets.
Unwilling to walk miles back
to the nearest bridge, I attempted
a crossing -- hoisted my pack
onto my head and stepped
into the muddy canal. I sank
to my right knee and panicked,
convinced another step forward
would suck me to the bottom.
Suddenly, a six-three drowning man
in a five-ten canal was no joke.
I threw my pack back to the bank,
turned, crawled onto ancestral ground.

Parklife

For Celeste

Most days after school we walked
to Victoria Park, where I pushed
you on the swings, spun you on the spinner,
launched you down the slope on the flying fox,
watched from a bench as you climbed
equipment I could never name,
took photos as you spun and soared.

Afterwards, you walked home balancing
on a stone wall beside the footpath
only holding my hand when unsteady,
moving freely between worlds,
unrestrained by boundaries and borders.

Icelandic Evening

For Tricia

Perusing local artworks in the domed gallery
of the Ásmundur Sveinsson Sculpture Museum

in a residential neighbourhood of Reykjavík
we immerse ourselves on a summer evening

in the unfamiliar, alter senses with abstractions,
portraits, landscapes, sculptures, installations,

Arctic Circle furniture and imported wine, climb
the spiral staircase, imbibe views across the city,

fill the frame with mountains, indigo and burgundy
rooftops, drink lava fields, swallow the North Atlantic.

Nativity

In a centuries-old English church
where Jane Austen worshipped,
my daughter performs her role
on the steps before the stone altar
in her school's nativity play
beneath stained-glass windows,
a star shining bright above
the road to Bethlehem,
a traveller from a foreign land
wearing the uniform of her peers,
accepted into the tribe,
lack of belief no impediment.

Rain Delay

For Celeste

The percussion of heavy rain
on our cosy blue tent woke us
before dawn on a June morning.
The ceaseless rain and the forecast
told us our Croagh Patrick climb must
be postponed until tomorrow.

Unwilling to risk the slick slopes
of the holy mountain or spend
the day huddled in our damp dome
we hustled to town through the grounds
of Westport House past dripping oaks
and soggy sheep in lush green fields.

Breakfasting in O'Cees on scones,
orange juice, croissants and coffee
we gazed through slanting rain at Saint
Patrick in the Octagon, hoping
silently for the downpour's end.
After browsing vinyl, fiction

and poetry in West Coast Rare
Books, buying the latest *Lockwood
& Co.* in McLoughlins, we ran
down James, crossed rushing Carrowbeg,
sheltered in the warm library,
reading and writing. After noon

we hurried through endless rain, drops
dripping from clothing, skin and hair,
to lunch at An File, relaxed
into a slow, snug afternoon
of soup, soda bread, smoked salmon,
chips, Guinness, lemonade and craic.

Americans

The Americans plod past
conspicuous as an unzipped fly

sighing and dragging excessive
luggage towards chain hotels

bulging bodies stuffed into
work-out clothes and running shoes

barely accustomed to walking
accents blaring like sirens

Maître D'

The maître d' stands outside
the restaurant's open doors
shirt untucked, sleeves rolled
waiting for diners to arrive

every few minutes he steps
inside and reaches behind
the door to the side table
where he keeps his rojo

takes a few sips to fortify himself
before stepping back into work
guiding lost tourists, chatting up
pretty girls, deploying his charm

running his hand over his finely
shaved head, spinning a pen
with thumb and forefinger
tapping the pen on his skull

in time to an invisible beat
glancing over his shoulder
to check for empty tables
as evening passes on the Corso

takes his wine into the street
stands with one hand pocketed
drinking and gazing, head turning
slowly to peruse passing women

Serenade

An old man in a straw hat
strolls down the middle of the street
playing an accordion and singing
Besame Mucho to the ladies
leaning on the balcony railings
high above, segues into *O Sole Mio*,
shouts greetings to individual
women between verses and choruses,
dances gracefully along the gutter
milking his silky baritone, hoping
for showers of applause and Euro.

In the Backstreet

On my hands and knees
in the backstreet

clutching the cobblestones
I found myself

slipping from consciousness
all over again

as bicycles rattled past
around the corner

and giggling couples
staggered towards clumsy

couplings after midnight
alone again losing skin

without pain
desperate to feel anything

to stop sliding downhill
in the backstreet

Tattooed

In your dream you encounter
a woman with the names

of her former lovers
tattooed across her breasts

she looks like an old friend
you almost seduced

Cave and Cohen

For Tricia

We spent a winter evening
reclining in front of the fire
listening to Cave and Cohen
working our way through glass
after glass of cabernet sauvignon

we sang along in whispers
as the kindling crackled
and the logs spat sparks
closed our eyes and escaped
into lyric-conjured universes

envisioned desperate men
trudging through snow
lamenting lost loves
in desolate landscapes
kneeling on stone church floors

dapper dark men in tailored suits
struggling to conquer grief
summoning beauty from darkness
crying out to a distant God
Eli, Eli, lema sabachthani?

Autumn Spring

Suddenly grandfatherless, I left Texas
spring on the daily non-stop QANTAS
flight, passed hours watching *Barracuda*
through waves of tears, listening to Ryan
Adams' *Prisoner* on repeat, lamenting
years not spent with family,
blunting the pain with Jameson's.

I touched down at Tullamarine,
embraced my parentless mother
and newly fatherless father,
drove straight to the Watergardens
to buy a black suit and SIM card.

I spent the time between my arrival
and the funeral with my parents
at Macedon, talking over tea,
running in the ranges through crisp
air and autumn leaves, driving through
the landscape of my formative
years to the town of my birth,
reminiscing over dinner and drinks
with relatives, sharing a rented
holiday house with parents and siblings.

On the morning of the funeral
jetlag woke me long before dawn.
I spent hours walking the streets
in darkness, stood on the beach
at sunrise, found myself outside
the hospital where I was born,
where Pa died just days before.

After the mass, the burial
and the wake, the carrying
of the coffin through the drizzle,
the conversations with uncles,
aunts and cousins accompanied
by beer and wine from Pa's birthplace,
the surprising joy of watching
cousins' children play, I drove to Melbourne
with my brother, spent four precious hours
conversing, stopped beside Lake Colac
to walk through the botanic gardens
in the rain, parted on the Spencer Street
bridge not knowing when we'd meet again.

Fresh from sprinkling dirt on my grandfather's
coffin, I spent the remains of the day
wandering Melbourne's glistening streets
and lanes in my black shoes, black tie and black
suit, wet with rain, immersing myself in home.

The next morning, I briefly returned
to my wife, daughter and life
in the northern hemisphere spring,
spent four days scaling exam mountains,
suffered the daily commute and parking
hunt, battled an inbox full of demands.

The academic year finally
complete, I crossed the Pacific
for the third time in nine days,
bound for an antipodean autumn
and weeks of solitude – time
enough to heal and create.

Hiraeth

Sunday afternoon reading Thomas
overwhelmed by hiraeth
remembering when we went down
to the shore young and easy

tumbling on the sand beside the waves
seagulls swirling overhead
pelicans gliding above their prey
sand in our hair and between our fingers

yearning for a time beyond time
when youth had no end
passion burned eternally
and death had no dominion

the grass on the sand dunes bent
beneath the force of the southerly
the crest of the waves blown to foam
the sky merging with the sea

(Un)belonging

Twenty-two years ago, I returned
from the northern
hemisphere for the first time

after two and a half years away,
escaped from a London winter
with snow on the ground

to a searing Melbourne summer.
I rode the bus to Canberra
to renew a distance-damaged

friendship. We drove north
from the bush capital to Bathurst.
Along the way I introduced

her to The Tragically Hip—
Road Apples and *Phantom Power*—
she gave me the gift of *Grace*.

We navigated drought-browned land,
through Gundaroo, Gunning and Gurrundah,
stopped to swim somewhere unnamed by settlers.

After Europe, the distance between towns
seemed immense, the land a nothingness,
my Anglo-Celtic skin foreign and ridiculous.

Taking turns driving, attempting reintegration,
I wondered if I could ever belong again
after so much time and distance.

In Bathurst, I slithered down the water-
slide at the public pool with the freckled
kids, swam laps while she sat in the shade,

rolled joints beside the back fence, smoked
behind gum trees. That evening, she joined
her choir performing Handel's *Messiah*

in a local church. I sat stoned in the gallery—
the closest to heaven I'd been in years.
We ditched the godbotherers

after the concert and drove down
to the Macquarie where we rolled
our own, talked into the early hours,

diminished the distance between
us, and finally drifted into dreams
beside the whispering river.

Booranga Sonnets

For Lachlan and David

Wagga Wagga

Proceed directly from the railway station
to Woolies. Buy a trolley full of groceries
and don't forget the vegies. Stock up
on beer, wine and whiskey at Dan Murphy's.
Walk the beach at the Murrumbidgee
with Mr. Wagga at sunset. Drink McLaren
Vale cabernet sauvignon at The Birdhouse
on Saturday evening before the student
production of *Hamlet*. Try to stay awake.
Sip a latte on Baylis Street like a resident
while tradies paste a four-metre-tall burger
to a restaurant wall as shoppers snap photos.
Watch workers lean from ladders smoothing
beef, cheese, lettuce and tomato across the scene.

Morning

Wake before dawn. Lie listening
for first birdsongs. Wonder how many
other writers have shared this bed,
heard these sounds, interpreted this space.
Take refuge from the autumn morning
in the steaming shower. Dress and pull
on two pairs of socks, slide across the lino
to the sink, fill and boil the kettle. Spoon
grounds into the French-press, add boiling
water, let coffee brew, watch steam rise,
depress the plunger and pour black liquid
into the blue glazed mug like the ones Nana
& Pa used on the Timboon farm. Turn
on Radio National. Follow weather.

Laundry

What I'd thought a fallen shirt
Under the line, flat on the grass
Was nothing but my shadow there,
Hinting that all things pass:
- Chris Wallace-Crabbe

Load the washing machine. Set
the water level to *medium*. Choose
warm-cold water temperature
and the *normal wash* cycle. Pull
the knob into the *on* position. Go
for a forty-minute walk in the bush.
If it's sunny, peg the washing outside
on the clothesline beside the house.
Open the windows, allow the breeze
to rustle book pages on the table.
On rainy days, plug in the electric
heater; assemble the clothes-rack;
drape damp socks, hankies, undies
and t-shirts on rungs beside the heat.

Evening

Turn on the electric heater at sunset.
Pour a generous glass of cabernet.
Cook spaghetti for one. Heat marinara
sauce and grate cheddar. Eat alone
at the round table in the kitchen.
Listen to rain insisting on the tin
roof. Wash the dishes by hand; let
them dry beside the sink. Pour another
glass of red. Move the heater closer
to the couch. Settle down with *Ned Kelly:
A Short Life*. Drink and read until drowsy.
Turn off the heater, brush teeth, crawl
beneath blankets, listen to the possum
crash around above the ceiling.

Bushwalk

Place your right palm on top
of the fence-post and swing each
leg in turn up and over the barbed
wire like a pommel-horse gymnast.
Climb the hill into the bush weaving
between lichen-covered boulders.
Pass beneath rustling gums and pines.
Dodge animal shit and fallen branches.
Beware the widow-makers. Stare down
the kangaroos pretending to be rocks.
Listen to the omnipresent buzz
of the bush. Observe the kookaburra
glide from tree to tree, laughing upon
arrival. Gain the summit and pause.

Running I

Slip into running clothes, tie shoe laces,
don beanie, stretch on the verandah.
Start off down the road as the sun rises,
exploring the local. Run past early-morning
olive-pickers shouldering supermarket bags
threatening to burst. Turn down Maybal
Lane, leap the locked gate like a ram,
pass flocks of sheep, lambs huddling
beside ewes, cows, magpies and crows.
Pass the vineyard remnant beside barbed-
wire fences, sheoaks, box and ghost gums.
Send flocks of cockatoos shrieking,
puff *morning!* harmlessly when passing
young women walking alone.

Running II

At the end of the lane, turn right
onto Coolamon Road and right again
at Farrer Road. Return past the new
housing estates, cramped embodiments
of the Australian Dream. Run through
thick fog as moisture drips from limbs,
boughs and leaves. Run down Pine Gully
Road through Estella and Boorooma.
Dig deep in the uphill homestretch
climbing Mambarra Drive to Booranga
past the RAF memorial, sheep-strewn
paddocks and the winery. Set lambs
bleating, mistake rocks for rabbits,
disturb many murders of crows.

Lunch

Heat up a can of beef and vegie
soup. Make four pieces of toast.
Generously spread Western Star
butter. Add Saxa salt and pepper
to the soup, open a longneck
of Sheaf Stout, pour a tall glass.
Eat and drink while gazing
out the window at a bloke
on a four-wheeler herding
a mob of sheep along the road,
pushing stragglers out of the olive
grove while the black cat meows
and scratches the fly-screen,
seeking entry from the verandah.

Afternoon

Brew your afternoon coffee
then step through the kitchen
doorway onto the verandah.
Watch the black cat dash down
the steps heading for home
beneath the house. Sit still
on a chair sipping in the autumn
sunshine. Stare at the rabbit
on the hillside until it turns
into a small grey rock then back
into a rabbit. Finish your coffee
and go inside. Iron trousers
and a long-sleeved shirt. Shave
in preparation for the reading.

Kangaroo

Stand at the kitchen sink washing dishes.
Stare at the rocks, boulders, grass, pine,
eucalyptus and olive trees on the hillside
until a kangaroo bounds past uphill. Step
outside for a better look as another Eastern
Grey rounds the corner of the house, jumps
the fence like it's invisible and heads uphill
following its companion. Hurdle the wires
and follow the roos between boulders,
ducking under olive-laden boughs. Surrender
the pursuit, climb the outcrop and look down
upon the house. Gaze across farmland
luxuriating in afternoon sunshine. Take selfies.
Capture the landscape's beauty over your shoulder.

Road Trip I

On the Urana-Lockhart road, slow
to twenty ks per hour when negotiating
roadworks; pass a worker wearing
a Green Bay Packers beanie and nod
as you glide by; gently spray fresh dirt
from borrowed tyres. Pass a grader
artfully smoothing the surface, sending
dirt curving into a berm. Acknowledge
the worker with a Ned Kelly beard
as he leans on his GO SLOW sign,
obeying orders. Reciprocate
when the local cop raises two fingers
on his right hand from the steering wheel
as he cruises by in his four-wheel-drive.

Road Trip II

Take the long way from Jerilderie to Wagga
via Griffith. Listen to Aussie hip-hop on Triple
J until the reception fades somewhere west
of Leeton. Read LUV U CHEEKIE spray-
painted on the back of a road sign beside
the Newell. Don't stop to take a photo
at Turn Back Jimmy Creek. Count dead roos
on the shoulder, including skeletons. Drive
past uncovered haystacks, irrigation channels,
vineyards, mandarin orchards, cotton fields,
grain silos, crows perched on fence posts.
Stop for a break in the Murrumbidgee Valley
National Park at Berry Jerry where parrots
and galahs burst from the bush like confetti.

Jerilderie

Eat a counter lunch of lamb shanks,
salad and chips at the Royal Mail Hotel
in the room where the Kelly Gang held
hostages. Wash it down with Kosciusko.
Examine the safe the Kelly's robbed.
Study the Kelly memorabilia on the walls
while the cook crashes about in the kitchen
shouting *bugger it!* Visit the former offices
of the *Jerilderie and Urana Gazette*, the Bank
of New South Wales, the Traveller's Rest,
the old Telegraph Office, the blacksmith's,
and Sir John Monash's childhood home.
Stop at the bakery and buy a latte, vanilla slice
and a poster-sized copy of the Jerilderie Letter.

Departure

Rise with the sun. Shower and dress.
Strip the bedsheets before breakfast.
Put on a load of linens and towels.
Pour juice. Make coffee and toast.
Wash and dry the breakfast dishes.
Hang the laundry on the line. Take
out the rubbish and the recycling.
Finish packing the suitcase and carry-on.
Check the drawers, wardrobe and under
the bed for overlooked items. Make sure
everything is where it belongs. Leave
the keys on the table. Lock the door.
Acknowledge the Wiradjuri. Remember
you are always a guest in this country.

Kengal

For Gary and David

On a Saturday afternoon in autumn
we climb The Rock and discuss past lives,
details of shearing, the current price per lamb,
the ten-year drought, virtues of various properties,
the lives of shearers and fruitpickers,

orchards in the Goulburn Valley,
roo-shooting in western New South Wales.
We climb higher through ironbark and cypress
past a Girl Scout troop, fitness-first families,
young couples staying sexy,

higher and higher, keeping an eye
out for Australian ravens, bimbins,
peewees and the elusive antechinus, climbing
between lichen-encrusted boulders
and sandy red rock, finally reaching the summit

to survey a spine of hills curving south,
green and brown fields, tree-lined roads,
dams, railway lines, the Olympic Highway,
blue skies smeared with vapour trails,
white clouds and distant towns—

Milbrulong, Tootool, Uranquinty,
Yerrong Creek, Mangoplah, Collingullie—
and the Murrumbidgee unfurling
westwards since time immemorial
through Wiradjuri country.

School Days

after Alan Wearne

I.

Callies & Kallies, Kellies & Kellys,
Jasons & Justins, Brents & Bretts
swamped the school during my years
wearing bottle-green woollen jumpers,
grey trousers, grey shirts, grey corduroy
Levi's, black Batas and elastic-sided boots.
The Cs and Ks and Js and Bs
controlled the cliques, ruled
over downball, cricket, basketball
and footy, decided Deb Ball
and party invitations, led the bullying
on the courts, on the fields,
in the change rooms, at the lockers,
behind the portables, in the classrooms,
on the bus, at the pool. Whether
you were in or out or somewhere
in between was up to the daily whims
of the Cs & Ks and Js & Bs.

II.

After school we rode our bikes
south through town down
the Goulburn Valley Highway
to hang out at the mall scarfing
a buck's worth of chips doused
with soy sauce, check out the girls
from Shepp High, Grammar
and Notre Dame, even the Kates,
Kristys, Sarahs and Sallys
who shared our classrooms.
On weekends and weeknights
we paid the price of admission
at the skating rink, bowling alley
and cinema, hoping for some
attention. Once we hit sixteen,
our mob of outcasts took to drinking
beside the Broken and the Goulburn,
staggered from pub to pub on Saturday
nights, attempted to avoid fights,
transcend the rituals and traps of country
town life, survive the final school days
before escaping to the big smoke.

Too Young

For Celeste

We killed time at the empty skate park
in Matamata, where I pretended
I had a board, running up the quarter-pipe
chucking one-eighties, sliding along
steel rails, simulating ollies and kickflips
while your mum toured hobbit holes.
Too young to be embarrassed,
you thought I was hilarious.

Worn out, we retired to a main street café
where we drank chocolate milk and a latte
while sharing an Anzac biscuit,
then drove until we found a playground.
You joined in with the Maori kids,
too young to know or care about race
or nationality, rolling down an embankment
into a pile of crunchy June leaves
while I exchanged nods with other dads.

When your mum returned from the tour
we took the narrow backroads in the rain
to Te Awamutu, hoping in vain to find
a monument to the Finns. We had to settle
for Waikato Draught at the Commercial Hotel.
You sipped lemonade, too young to understand
why we cared about music from New Zealand.

Saronic

I read Cavafy on Vouliagmenis
beach while my daughter snorkels,
chasing yellow and white fish
amongst elderly floaters
and kids in inflatable rings.

Teenage girls stand motionless
in the water keeping hair
and make-up perfect
while middle-aged men in Speedos
swim out to the buoys.

Women and girls of all ages
lie flat on loungers angled
towards the sun. Coconut
oil scents the breeze.

My Aphrodite lies topless,
wonders aloud why Greek
women aren't baring breasts
like the French, Italians,
Spanish and Germans.

Yachts and pleasure cruisers
rest moored at the marina.
Passenger jets pass overhead
between Athens and the islands.

We bake beneath a cloudless
sky, chase umbrella shade,
scan the beach for exotic
scenes as shadows of seagulls
pass across the white sand.

Locals secure towels to sunbeds
with plastic clips, defeat the wind.

I sip Alpha as it turns warm
and kids with fish and water
in a plastic bag yell excitedly
in a language I don't recognize.

Pigeons strut beneath sunbeds
towards the water as teenage boys
play football shirtless on the grass
behind the beach, flaunting
their lack of body fat.

An elderly lady lying facedown
gives herself a wedgie with both
hands to increase the expanse
of buttocks exposed to the sun.

A twentysomething man massages
the tattooed neck of his partner
while a man with his right arm
in a sling watches a pale middle-aged
man write in a pocket-sized notebook.

A car alarm beseeches from the distance
while my neighbour answers his wife's
questions with *nai, nai, nai*.

I pour a pool of sunscreen
onto my expanding belly,
rub it in with circular strokes.

Beach-neighbours greet each other
with *yia sas* and *kalimera*, exchange
handshakes and kisses
as I drain my last Alpha.

Flags flutter above the lifeguards'
tower indicating winds blowing
straight out into the gulf
towards the distant isles.

At the beach bar a woman
half my age barely wearing
a bikini approaches the bartender
with a phone charger, leans over
the counter, makes her request.
The bartender shrugs, peruses
her body, jokes with his co-worker,
plugs the charger in with a flourish
as the supplicant swafts away.

I swim out past the buoys
into the azure, dive to the bottom,
hold my breath while sailboarders
race each other across the deep.

A teenage boy rubs sunscreen
into the back of a teenage girl's
upper thighs, takes his sweet time
while she reads texts on her phone.

An Adonis rolls his shorts all the way
up, maximising his tan, lies on his back,
legs spread wide, left hand caressing
his girlfriend's back and arse.

My Athena sleeps facedown
in the sun, salt seasoning skin
as the pock-pock of paddle-tennis
matches travels from the grass
behind the sand towards the sea.

Between sandcastle construction
frenzies, our daughter reads *Flyte*,
escapes into fantastic worlds
as I switch from Alpha to Mythos.

An elderly woman wearing a bikini
and high-heeled sandals attempts
to sashay to the water's edge,
almost attains grace.

Couples and families arrive,
search for prime waterfront
real estate while two Englishmen
take up a position at my rear.

The mother of my daughter
eases herself into the Saronic
in a pink and black bikini,
ties back her long brown hair,
captures Mediterranean male gazes.

Three twentysomething men
share a sunbed, huddle together,
skin touching, watch football
stream through an iPhone.

Four bronzed bearded men ride
an inflatable pink flamingo over
foot-high waves, laugh and gesticulate,
revel in pure childish pleasure.

Young couples faux-wrestle and kiss
in the shallows, eager for the touch
of bare wet skin, as my Artemis
emerges from the water like Ursula
Andress, resolves to finish her novel.

Return Flight

Tired sunburned passengers
flying home from vacations

puzzle over Sudoku and crosswords
doze against strangers' shoulders

read thrillers and airline magazines
grudgingly answer email on laptops

watch *Game of Thrones* on iPads
draw pictures of *Harry Potter* characters

pray that the big guy doesn't recline
snack on mini pretzels

sip coffee and orange juice
retract elbows, shoulders and feet

to evade the drinks cart
and wide-hipped passengers

charging down the aisle
doze off with nodding heads

startle themselves awake with snorts
escort kids to the toilets

curse the airline for lack of legroom
and exorbitant alcohol prices

scroll through photos on phones
searching for elusive images

capturing the happiest, most exciting
and beautiful moments

editing the decent and deleting the crap
like revisionist historians

Ash Wednesday

A pastor loiters on the lawn
beside the sidewalk outside
the Methodist Campus Ministry

left hand in his pocket, right
hand clutching a brown glazed
bowl of ashes beside a poster

attached to a wooden easel
with a hand-written message
in thick blue ink: ASHES & PRAYERS

students rush past the pastor
on their way to class, focus eyes
on iPhones, cracks in the pavement

passing trucks, bikes and cars
buildings under construction
muddy water flowing in the gutter

Blackout

Students arrive in rainboots,
waterproof jackets, dripping,
tuck wet hair behind ears,

brush strands from mouths,
drape jackets over chairbacks.
Raindrops beat on stained carpet

like the clock's second hand.
Dark skies outside windows
dull the room's mood, drain

energy from young brains
like dementors sucking souls.
Thunder vibrates windowpanes,

startles the girl in the corner,
spills Starbucks across her desk,
books, yoga pants and backpack.

Winds force boughs of live oaks
against the glass, scraping
and scratching like Cathy's nails

while the chapel bell tolls
the hour across glistening lawns
until lightning strikes, cuts power.

Mort

My friends' parents
are dying

finally
we've reached that awful age

separated from death
by a single fragile generation

another parent
was taken last night

thankfully
in his sleep

soon nothing
will stand between us

and death

Pond Frog

a young frog makes its home
in the backyard pond

beneath the stone water feature
unaware that every summer

for the past five years other frogs
have lived in the same pond

until consecutive hundred-degree
days heat the water to the precise

temperature at which frogs die
and float to the surface

Alt-facts Bio

My favourite subject at school was physics.
I always wanted to drive a monster truck.

I play the harp, pennywhistle and bodhran.
I keep a rabbit's foot in my pocket for luck.

I am six foot six, my hair lustrous and black.

I speak fluent Farsi, Mandarin and Icelandic
and can order beer, ouzo and gyros in Greek.

I ran the Reykjavik marathon in two hours
and twenty minutes, setting a course record.

My first wife was Elle McPherson.
I traded her in for a newer model.

I scored a triple-century on debut for Australia
during the Boxing Day test at the MCG.

1.25 million people attended my graduation
and gave a forty-five-minute standing ovation.

Escape Sonnet

Follow the HURRICANE EVACUATION ROUTE
north away from the Gulf Coast to Fort Worth
past new subdivisions metastasizing
beyond Houston on freshly-bulldozed earth
carved out of the woodlands with beautiful
new floorplans from the low 100s
past the giant statue of Sam Houston
forever standing guard beside the Interstate
past the Texas Prison Museum
in Huntsville, ignoring the billboard
advertising the electric chair
past Woody's Smokehouse in Centreville
where the pits are always smoking
through Buffalo, Corsicana and Waxahachie

Refuge

On Willow Bend Drive
in the last open field

behind the strip mall
beside the medical center

a white-tail doe and her fawn
pause at the street's edge

before clicking across concrete
to the last stand of live oak

Nonchalance

An overweight, elderly man
lights a cigarette as he walks
across the medical center
parking lot, takes four or five
drags while he ambles,
throws the lit cigarette forward
onto the ground with his right hand,
pauses, grinds it out with his right foot,
proceeds onwards towards automatic
doors and the doctor's diagnosis.

Decay

Two pairs of white canvas shoes,
laces tied together, hang from powerlines
high above the entrance to the subdivision
like a warning against suburban dreams.

The empty shell of a Jacuzzi lies
stranded on its side beside the Interstate:
abandoned, waterless, motorless.

Three miles closer to the city
a king-sized mattress sleeps
on the shoulder, pillow-top torn,
stuffing emerging like a hernia.

Pecos

Hike along the Pecos River
through the Pecos River Canyon

climb through stands
of pine, birch and spruce

follow the path beside the river
watch chipmunks, rabbits and deer

traverse high mountain meadows
through millions of butterflies

glimpse snow surviving
through high summer on Truchas Peak

climb cliffs, jump from rocks
bathe in the river at Dalton Canyon

let clear cold mountain water
wake you and wash you clean

Ice Cream Social

At Ken's Ice Cream on Route 66
in Tucumcari, New Mexico,
we meet a retired couple
from Birmingham traversing
the mother road, unperturbed
by the decay, the boarded-up
abandoned motels, gas stations,
diners, restaurants and bars,
possessing the ability to see
past the present into the past,
to ignore depressing reality
and envision the glory days.
We sit in adjoining booths,
talk about shared experiences,
learn that we were in the same
English town last New Year's
Eve and agree that the bloody
rain ruined everything. We share
travel recommendations, compare
notes on theme parks, hotels, cities
and towns from L.A. to Chicago
as we eat our ice cream. After
the last sweet drops are licked
from fingers we shake hands,
part without exchanging
names, resume our journeys
into the past and the future.

Swinging

from the rope
I drop into the pool
like a fearless teenager

falling into a country
river
on a mate's dare

racing my daughter
underwater
I nearly let her win

I am at home
in the shade
sipping cerveza

watching my love
float on her raft chilled
white wine in hand

The Third of July

On the corner of Prairie Dunes
and Spyglass sixteen miniature
American flags line the path

to the police officer's door.
Two neighbors mow lawns
but most have left town

or gone to church to hear
the annual patriotic sermon.
At the corner of Bayhill

and Spyglass a Mayflower
moving truck swings wide
forcing me to leave the street

and cross someone's lawn,
the driver failing to offer
an apologetic wave.

High above, fighter jets
from the Air Force base
rehearse for the next war.

Back Verandah Dinner

For Tricia

Knives slice maple-glazed brussel
sprouts cut into peppered steaks

glasses transport chilled
pinot grigio to lips

bees settle inside flowers
robins twitter and flutter

hummingbirds hover while feasting
on the fruit of the trumpet vine

the breeze rotates the back
verandah ceiling fan

water trickles over rocks
into the frog-free pond

open hands wave flies
away from plates and glasses

your leg rests against mine
transmitting warmth

As He Lies Dying

In memoriam Peter George O'Reilly (1927-2017)

In another hemisphere, across half a continent
and an ocean, my grandfather lies dying.
I am unable to hold his hand, kiss his forehead,
share a longneck of Carlton Draught, say

Remember when your bull
almost gored me at Timboon?
I should have listened to you
and stayed on the tractor.

My daughter loves the painting
of the galah you gave her
last time we visited, before
we had to put you in the home.

The Jerilderie Letter
is pure Irish bush poetry.

I often recall the taste
of the molasses you gave me
from the bucket in the dairy
after milking at Timboon.

You never told me your favourite
Slim Dusty song. I never cared
that I didn't catch any fish
when you took me fishing
at Logan's beach. I just wanted
to watch you cast out beyond
the breaking waves, reel in whiting
after whiting as if they were waiting
for you to bring them home.

I always admired the way
you broke the necks
of the kittens we found
in the hessian sack
beside the rubbish bin
in the beach car park.
You were stoic in your mercy,
but I saw the tear before
you erased it with the back
of your sun-damaged hand.

Beach Ballet

In the midst of an Irish heatwave,
lying on a longboard in the swale
at Lahinch chatting with a Paul Kelly

lookalike between sets, I look over
my right shoulder towards the beach
and watch a tween girl catch a wave,

rise to her feet, balance gracefully,
knees bent, arms wide and relaxed,
ride all the way to the shallows

before stepping lightly off the side
of the board into knee-deep foam.
The girl's ride is almost complete

before I recognize her as my daughter,
just twenty minutes into her first lesson,
adapting, evolving, becoming herself.

Afterword

I was born in Warrnambool on Gunditjmara country, a descendant of convicts & immigrants from Ireland, England, Wales & Portugal. My ancestors farmed in the Western District of Victoria & the McLaren Vale of South Australia on stolen land. I've always felt like an outsider & struggled to attain belonging. I left Australia when I was twenty-two & have lived overseas for more than half my life. I have multiple homelands & hometowns but don't fully belong anywhere. The poems in this collection are creations of my experiences, relationships, beloved places & obsessions: hybridity, distance, alienation, homesickness; landscapes, hiraeth, border crossings & hedgerows; international flights; death, suburbia, mountain forests, bushwalks, Irish music & grasslands; the Western District, sand dunes, islands, volcanic rock, bluestone walls & twilight; marriage & fatherhood; nuclear & extended families; Australia, Ireland, America, England, Greece, Iceland, Italy & New Zealand; Portland, Fort Worth, Melbourne, Dublin, Galway, Wagga, Paris, Florence, Reykjavík, Athens, Warrnambool, Port Fairy, Ballarat & Shepparton; live oaks & magnolias; campus lawns; cemeteries full of grandparents, great-grandparents & great-great grandparents; ancestors' surnames; the Grand Canal; cobblestone-paved laneways; water; ancestral homelands; exile; endless rain; shelter; accents & identity; invisibility; gazing & observing; backstreets; dreams & nostalgia; memories & forgetting; escape; grief & beauty; autumn leaves; driving through landscapes; running, walking, climbing, swimming & surfing; carrying coffins; Atlantic & Pacific crossings; lost youth; yearning; beaches & rivers; departure & return; trams, trains, planes, boats & ships; enlightenment; hills & mountains; fog; verandas & eucalyptus; home.

Notes

The epigraphs are from Seamus Heaney's 'Postscript' (*100 Poems*, Faber & Faber, 2018) and 'A Herbal' (*Human Chain*, Farrar, Straus & Giroux, 2010).

'Your Gaze' is partially inspired by Gerald Murnane's *The Plains* (Norstrilia Press, 1982).

'O My America!': the last three lines of the poem are adapted from John Donne's 'Elegy XX: To His Mistress Going to Bed.'

'Well Tempered' was co-written with Lachlan Brown and is based on experiences in Wagga, Fort Worth, Portland, Paris and Sydney. The poem previously appeared in *Collaboration*, edited by Louis Armand and Helen Lambert, a special issue of *Cordite Poetry Review* published in 2014. Big thanks to Lachlan for allowing me to include the poem in this book.

'The Confessions of Donald J. Trump': all text taken from Trump's press conference on February 16th, 2017.

'Grand Canal Drowning': the first stanza includes a story my great-uncle Sean Quigley told me in Dublin in 1996. The second stanza owes a small debt to U2's 'Drowning Man,' from the album *War* (Island, 1983).

'Parklife' borrows its title from Blur's album of the same name (SBK, 1994).

'Rain Delay': I borrowed the phrase 'endless rain' from James' song 'Sometimes,' which appears on *Laid* (Mercury, 1993). The name of the pub, An File, is Irish for 'the poet.' The pub, located in Westport, Ireland, is named for the famed blind poet Antoine Ó Raifteirí (1779-1835).

'Cave and Cohen': the last line of the poem is from Matthew 27:46 – 'Around the ninth hour, Jesus shouted in a loud voice, saying 'Eli, Eli, lema sabachthani?' The English translation of the Aramaic is 'My God, my God, why have you forsaken me?'

'Hiraeth' contains two lines adapted from Dylan Thomas' poems 'And death shall have no dominion' and 'Fern Hill.' 'Hiraeth' is a Welsh word referring to nostalgia, homesickness and a deep longing for home.

'(Un)belonging': The poem refers to two albums by The Tragically Hip, *Road Apples* (MCA, 1991) and *Phantom Power* (Universal, 1998), and Jeff Buckley's *Grace* (Columbia, 1994).

Booranga Sequence: early drafts of the poems in the sequence were written on Wiradjuri country while I was the writer-in-residence at Booranga Writers' Centre in May of 2017. I acknowledge and pay respect to the Wiradjuri, the traditional owners and custodians of the land on which the poems were written, and to their elders, past, present and future. The epigraph to 'iii. Laundry' in the Booranga Sequence is from Chris Wallace-Crabbe's 'At the Clothesline,' part of his sequence 'The Domestic Sublime,' published in his collection *Telling a Hawk from a Handsaw* (Carcanet, 2008).

'Blackout' borrows its title from U2's song 'The Blackout,' which appears on *Songs of Experience* (Interscope, 2017).

'Beach Ballet': the phrase 'stepping lightly' is borrowed from Van Morrison's song 'Ballerina,' which appears on *Astral Weeks* (Warner Bros., 1968).

Acknowledgments

Special thanks to Lachlan Brown for his feedback on earlier versions of the poems in this book, and to Shane Strange for giving my work detailed, honest and insightful editorial attention. I'm delighted and honored to have Recent Work Press as my publisher. I'm extremely grateful to Booranga Writers' Centre, Charles Sturt University, Arts NSW, Wagga Wagga City Council and Griffith City Library for a writing residency, book launch and readings during May of 2017; massive thanks to David Gilbey and Kathryn Halliwell for the opportunity and their incredible hospitality. Deepest gratitude to Poetry Ireland, Galway's Over the Edge Reading Series, the Limerick Writers' Centre, Cork's Ó Bhéal Reading Series, Anne Casey, Eleanor Hooker, Kevin Bateman, Kevin Higgins, Dominic Taylor, Paul Casey, Edward O'Dwyer, Shona Blake, Anne Rynne, Claire Watts and Ali Whitelock for the June/July 2018 reading tour of Ireland. The words, music, hospitality and craic will stay with me for the rest of my days. Big thanks to Kit Kelen for inviting me to join Project 366 in mid-2016; I'm tremendously grateful to Kit and my fellow participants who read and commented on my work daily for a month. Thanks also to Tricia Jenkins, Celeste Jenkins-O'Reilly, Paul & Moira O'Reilly, Sean Scarisbrick, Penny Ingram, Cedrick May, Jeremy Bennett, Heather Hornor, David & Lisa Bonnet, Toby Davidson, Peter Mathews, Nicholas Birns, Patrick Stack, Derek Motion, Michelle D'Souza, Annemarie Ní Churreáin, Stuart Barnes, Mark Roberts, Dan Disney, Kent McCarter, David McCooey, Paul Kane, Michele Seminara, Robbie Coburn, Aidan Coleman, Thom Sullivan, Jonathan Bennett, Lyn McCredden, David Adès, Katherine Gallagher, Stephen Matthews, Terri-ann White, Jessica Hepburn, Alex Lemon, Curt Rode, Jason Helms, Matthew Pitt, T.J. McLemore, Chantel Langlinais Carlson, Rima Abunasser, Joddy Murray, Bonnie Blackwell, Sarah Robbins, Brad Lucas, Mark Nobles, Libby Charlton, Ross Bramley, Grant Ferrier, Nadya Peshevska, Tanya Vaughan, Broose Dickinson, the Haltons and Hoods of Bath, and my O'Reilly clan in Australia for love, friendship, encouragement, opportunities and inspiration.

Many of the poems in this collection have been published previously, sometimes in a slightly different form. I am grateful to the editors of the following publications: *Adelaide Literary Magazine, Anthropocene, Antipodes, Backstory, Bluepepper, Cordite Poetry Review, fourW twenty-eight, fourW thirty, FourXFour, Glasgow Review of Books, Ink, Sweat & Tears, Marathon Literary Review, Mascara Literary Review, The Newcastle Poetry Prize Anthology 2017, A New Ulster, Nothing Substantial, Other Terrain, PRISM, Red River Review, Rochford Street Review, Skylight 47, Social Alternatives, Taj Mahal Review* and *Transnational Literature*.

About the author

Nathanael O'Reilly was born in Warrnambool in 1973 and grew up in Ballarat, Brisbane and Shepparton. He attended university at Monash and Ballarat before moving overseas. He has travelled on five continents and spent extended periods in England, Ireland, Germany, Ukraine and the United States. He is the author of *Preparations for Departure* (UWAP Poetry, 2017), named one of the '2017 Books of the Year' in *Australian Book Review*; *Distance* (Picaro Press, 2014; Ginninderra Press, 2015); and the chapbooks *Cult* (Ginninderra Press, 2016), *Suburban Exile* (Picaro Press, 2011) and *Symptoms of Homesickness* (Picaro Press, 2010). O'Reilly received an Emerging Writers Grant from the Literature Board of the Australia Council for the Arts in 2010 and was writer-in-residence at Booranga Writers' Centre in May 2017. His poems have appeared in journals and anthologies in twelve countries, including *Adelaide Literary Magazine, Antipodes, Australian Love Poems, Backstory, Cordite Poetry Review, FourW, FourXFour, Glasgow Review of Books, Headstuff, Mascara Literary Review, Other Terrain, Postcolonial Text, Skylight 47, Snorkel, Tincture, Transnational Literature, Verity La* and *The Newcastle Poetry Prize Anthology 2017*. He has given readings in Australia, Canada, England, Hungary, Ireland, Italy and the United States.

www.ingramcontent.com/pod-product-compliance
Lightning Source LLC
Chambersburg PA
CBHW020329010526
44107CB00054B/2030